THE
E-COMMERCE
POCKETBOOK

Will Rowan

Drawings by Phil Hailstone

"...y two copies of this book: one for you and one for your boss. It's an exceptionally ...to-understand guide for executives just beginning to do business online."
... Holland, Publisher, http://www.MarketingSherpa.co.uk
(...United Kingdom's Leading "How-To" Weekly on Internet Marketing)

"...seful and helpful guide to the basic principles of e-commerce. For the beginner or ...all business, it gives a clear steer on the key issues to consider before moving online. ...ll written and very clear, it's a handy guide for the uninitiated."
...essor Der... Hol... Warwickshire College ...stitute of Direct Marketing

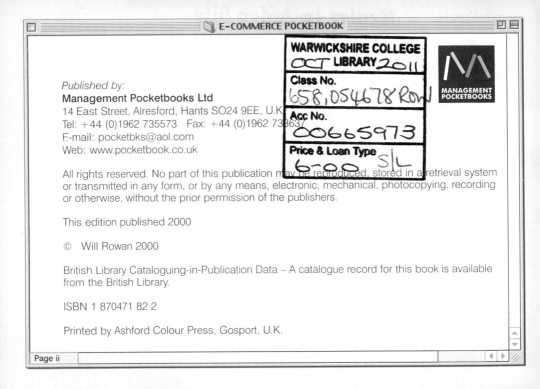

Published by:
Management Pocketbooks Ltd
14 East Street, Alresford, Hants SO24 9EE, U.K.
Tel: +44 (0)1962 735573   Fax: +44 (0)1962 733637
E-mail: pocketbks@aol.com
Web: www.pocketbook.co.uk

This edition published 2000

© Will Rowan 2000

British Library Cataloguing-in-Publication Data – A catalogue record for this book is available from the British Library.

ISBN 1 870471 82 2

Printed by Ashford Colour Press, Gosport, U.K.

FROM THE AUTHOR

What to expect in this book

This book can be used as a series of quick reference guides on particular topics. Or read it from end to end as a development programme for an online business. Whichever you choose, it is full of sound ideas that make online businesses more profitable.

As the web is the most developed of the online technologies, I've made sure that all of the ideas can be applied to internet websites. Most of them can also be applied to other, emerging online channels. So, where the text refers to the internet and websites, in time the same will apply to interactive television, mobile telephones and who knows what other network devices.

Where to go next

Each section ends with an Action Plan. These are short templates to help identify, separate and prioritise important and urgent issues. For more advice and real-life experiences, join fellow readers online at: www.ecommercepocketbook.com

Will Rowan

CONTENTS

WHAT IS E-COMMERCE? 1
A moment of calm, what not to expect, drivers of e-commerce, growth of online population, 7 things to know and 8 things to do

THE FIVE BUSINESS BENEFITS OF E-COMMERCE 11
Cost reduction, measurement, interactivity, personalisation, global reach

NEW THINKING FOR ONLINE BUSINESS 29
High street vs online market, viral campaigning, harvesting e-mail addresses, be first and stay ahead, market spaces

HOW TO PROMOTE A COMPANY ONLINE 47
Four levels of commitment to being online, different ways to use e-mail for marketing, online public relations, online advertising

MANAGING SEARCH ENGINES 73
What are search engines, using a URL, meta tags, keywords, alt tags

CREATING TRUST: SECURITY & DATA PROTECTION 89
Appropriate security, 5 ways to build trust and 6 ways to lose it, domain names, data protection, personal privacy issues, contracts and the law

EIGHT STEPS TO PLAN SUCCESSFUL E-COMMERCE 111
Let customers decide, respond fast, test plan, challenge assumptions, focus on benefits, encourage visitors, understand cost implications, help staff adapt

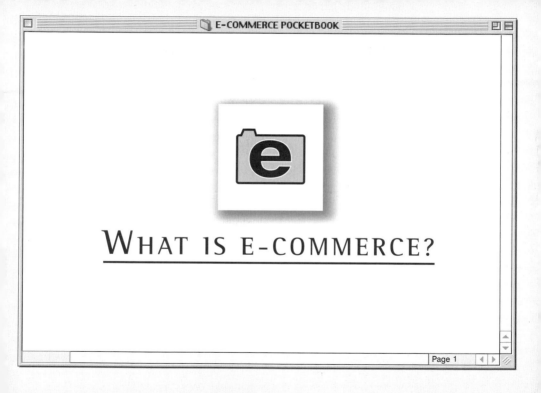

WHAT IS E-COMMERCE?

WHAT IS E-COMMERCE?

A MOMENT OF CALM IN THE RUSH TO A NETWORKED, ONLINE WORLD

In the rush to digitise businesses, it's all too easy to forget that the human beings this side of the screen won't change much. Some have adapted early and have already leapt online. Others will take longer.

And some of us will never wish to go online.

In the dash to offer online services to your customers, never forget that some of them just don't want to come and play.

"WHERE IS EVERYONE?"

WHAT IS E-COMMERCE?

WHAT NOT TO EXPECT

- ↗ Don't expect to gain an advantage *just by being online*
- ↗ Don't dress up an existing business with a dot.com façade
- ↗ Don't use it as an alternative to investing in sound customer service
- ↗ Don't think only of reaching the internet on a PC: our telephones and televisions can already be networked
- ↗ Don't take short cuts; it might look the same but won't get the same results

And don't expect:

- ↗ E-commerce to happen quietly, in a corner, over there behind the shrubbery
- ↗ To keep the rest of your business unchanged
- ↗ To be an overnight success

WHAT IS E-COMMERCE?

WHAT'S DRIVING THE GROWTH OF E-COMMERCE?

Every day more people are online - at home and at work, via computers, telephones and televisions. These devices are becoming faster, smarter and are connecting to each other.

For many items that we need to buy, both domestic and commercial, online is a more convenient way of shopping.

The businesses that sell to us can reduce their costs, making each sale more profitable.

WHAT IS E-COMMERCE?

A DEFINITION OF E-COMMERCE

 By connecting to a standardised network we can find information, buy and sell quickly and easily, with lower process and administration costs.

WHAT IS E-COMMERCE?

WHAT'S GROWING THE ONLINE POPULATION?

The cost of being connected is falling, fast.

Moore's Law holds that every 18 months computing power halves in cost (or doubles in power). This means that we get mobile telephones with more computing power than ten-year old computers.

Almost every computing device is connected to a network - wired into an office network or connected to the internet.

Very soon it will be commonplace for non-computing devices to be networked in the same way. From cars to fridges, we'll live and work in a networked economy.

WHAT IS E-COMMERCE?

WHAT'S GROWING THE ONLINE POPULATION?

Connection speeds are rising.

The telephone network was designed to carry voice calls. Now the majority of traffic is not voice but data calls.

When you connect to the internet your download speed will depend on the speed of your modem and on how busy the lines are. If you are connecting through a voice line, the bandwidth is limited. Connect through a line designed to take data and you will enjoy almost instant downloads.

WHAT IS E-COMMERCE?

FOR READERS WORKING TO INTERNET TIME*

7 things to know about e-commerce

1. Online, space is practically infinite; the value of space falls as the supply rises

2. Successful e-commerce takes costs out of business processes

3. It's possible to be open 24/7/365

4. Distance disappears when connections are electronic and online

5. Company size is not a competitive advantage when everybody is on the same screen

6. Heritage, and the customer perceptions it brings, may be a disadvantage

7. Relationships matter even more online

 Internet time is said to run seven times faster. One internet month, therefore, is equivalent to seven 'real' months

WHAT IS E-COMMERCE?

FOR READERS WORKING TO INTERNET TIME

8 things to do

1. Take costs out of your existing business
2. Improve your internal communications
3. Build a community and get knowledge to flow freely inside and outside your company
4. Make external communications more cost-effective
5. Find more efficient ways to reach existing customers
6. Take orders 24 hours a day
7. Exploit the opportunities created by being closer to all of your customers
8. Try out new markets with less risk

And one thing not to do ..... **don't bet the company on an online venture.**

THE FIVE BUSINESS BENEFITS OF E-COMMERCE

THE FIVE BUSINESS BENEFITS OF E-COMMERCE

BENEFITS AT A GLANCE

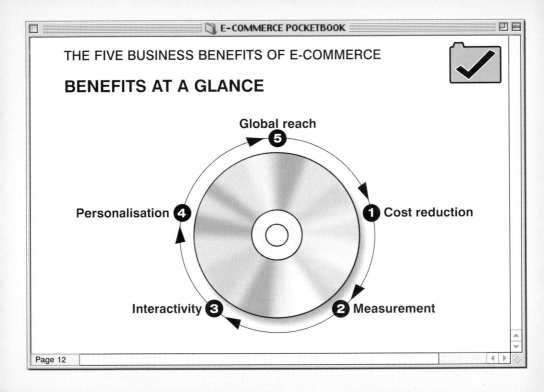

THE FIVE BUSINESS BENEFITS OF E-COMMERCE

1. COST REDUCTION

Reduce the cost of doing business - it's the benefit.

So-called *frictionless* trade benefits the entire business by getting computers to handle processing and information tasks for your whole business, online and offline.

Information need only be entered into a system once. In that case it had better be correct. Your customers are the best people to get much of the information onto your systems correctly, first time. We all know how to spell our own details and it matters to us that they're right.

Therefore, use the internet to save money by out-sourcing data entry to your customers.

But beware of using e-commerce only to save money.

1 Cost reduction

THE FIVE BUSINESS BENEFITS OF E-COMMERCE

1. COST REDUCTION

Beware of using e-commerce only to save money. Yes, I said that on the previous page so it must be important.

Reinvest your savings in *customer service* because:

↗ The web's transparency means that inadequate service shows up fast.

↗ Your customers' expectations will change. When they can't find information for themselves online, they'll want answers quickly from your support staff.

↗ Bad news can travel very fast online: a web community can let a whole industry know of a problem, quickly.

Aim for faster customer service and move it online for greater cost-effectiveness.

Develop online self-help customer service for simple, routine questions. Save staff resources for tougher, one-off customer concerns.

Be prepared to re-train your customer service teams. They will be answering much more detailed questions from your online customers.

THE FIVE BUSINESS BENEFITS OF E-COMMERCE

2. MEASUREMENT

Online, everything can be measured.

Everything that happens online can be tracked, counted and measured. The details are usually held in a log file* available from the host** computer. This is a goldmine of information on how your customers use your online channels:

↗ Who came in and the website they came from

↗ The route they took around the site

↗ The products they looked at and the products they bought

This information is virtually free to collect. The challenge is to find the information that will inform management decisions.

* *A log file reports (logs) activity on your website.*

** *The host computer stores your website. It is often an internet service provider or another host. In the case of an interactive TV channel, the TV provider will host the site.*

THE FIVE BUSINESS BENEFITS OF E-COMMERCE

2. MEASUREMENT

Measure site traffic for quantity and quality.

Do you have plenty of online visitors? Are they the right people?

Most visitors will not tell you exactly who they are, unless they need more information from you.

But you will be able to see:

- ↗ Where in the world they came from
- ↗ Which internet service providers are most common: local, national or international
- ↗ What time of day your site is busiest

Don't mistake a high volume of traffic for valuable traffic. What use are overseas shoppers if you only deliver locally? They will only soak up valuable company resources that you need for local customers.

THE FIVE BUSINESS BENEFITS OF E-COMMERCE

2. MEASUREMENT

Measure site traffic for quantity and quality.

How did your visitors find you? Websites sit on servers whose log files have all the traffic reports that are needed to analyse and manage the flow of visitor traffic through a site.

Do you know them already?

- ↗ Is it their first visit or are they returning?
- ↗ Did they use a bookmark or did they find you through a search engine?
- ↗ What search terms did they use?

Are you ready for them?

- ↗ How is their computer set up?
- ↗ Which browser* and which version are they using?
- ↗ Are they seeing your pages as you meant them to? What are the most popular screen resolution settings?

★ *Browsers are the programs used to view the web. Microsoft's Internet Explorer, Netscape's Navigator and the AOL browser are the most common. There are PC and Macintosh versions of each.*

THE FIVE BUSINESS BENEFITS OF E-COMMERCE

2. MEASUREMENT

Measure the routes taken by visitors.

Did they find what they were looking for?

Which was the first (entry) page to your site? Search engines won't always lead surfers to your home page. If one page is particularly popular, try to understand why.

What are the most popular routes? Which pages do visitors link together? Is that where you want them to go? If it isn't, where is the smartest place to put a signpost link, to redirect the traffic flow?

Stickiness: which pages do visitors spend most time on? Was it: finding product information, filling out forms and placing orders? Do they spend seconds or several minutes on these pages?

Is there a popular *last page visited*? What route do most visitors take when leaving your site? With luck, it will be the order page. But you're probably not lucky. Track back visitors' routes to the exit pages. Change the links and signposts to re-route them towards preferred exit pages.

THE FIVE BUSINESS BENEFITS OF E-COMMERCE

3. INTERACTIVITY

Human beings are naturally curious. We like picking up stones to see what's underneath, and we like clicking buttons and switches to see what happens. Websites are great at interactivity. Use them to create immediate interest for your visitors. Have your visitors interact with your pages, to enable them to find the information that's really relevant to them today.

Interactivity **3**

By clicking, visitors *engage* and involve themselves in discovering your products. In this way they'll spend longer at your site*, and will tell you more about their interests through the pages that they look at.

Beware, too many flashing, rotating graphics are distracting. Pages should communicate first and entertain second.

★   *Stickiness is the webspeak for this.*

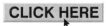

THE FIVE BUSINESS BENEFITS OF E-COMMERCE

3. INTERACTIVITY

Interactivity drives personalisation.

Isn't it nice when we visit a shop and are greeted by name? We feel recognised and valued. Online, this applies too.

Shopkeeper: *Hi. Have you been before?*

Customer: *No* (most likely response since the web is a new medium and many people are new online).

Shopkeeper: *Let me give you the grand tour. Or was there something specific I can get for you?*

Alternatively, the customer answers *yes* to the original question, in which case the shopkeeper says: *What did you like? Can I show you that first next time?*
In this way the shopkeeper is given **permission** to get into conversation with the customer about who they are and what goods they like.

THE FIVE BUSINESS BENEFITS OF E-COMMERCE

4. PERSONALISATION

Personalisation works for me.

Now that our customer is engaged in conversation the shopkeeper can ask the questions that drive personalisation. It's the first step to *free*, accurate data collection. To encourage visitors to give their names, use the data that they supply. There is no point asking for information that won't be used and won't be useful.

There are three levels to personalisation:

- ↗ **Recognition** can save re-entering names and invoice and delivery addresses in order forms. This saves time and is convenient for customers.

- ↗ Using software, the site can be **personalised** for the customer according to his or her past site activities.

- ↗ The most advanced level is **customisation**. Customers can choose how and when they view the site's content.

Personalisation ❹

When visitors feel valued, they will return more frequently and stay longer each time.

THE FIVE BUSINESS BENEFITS OF E-COMMERCE

4. PERSONALISATION

Recognition: manual customer log-in.

If you are online you'll almost certainly have an e-mail address. E-mail addresses are the best means to recognise visitors to your website. Moreover, they provide a convenient way in which to send information to your contacts. It makes sense, therefore, to try to capture - harvest - visitors' e-mail addresses. For a good harvest, present visitors with sound reasons to submit their e-mail addresses. For example, tempt them with a newsletter, product updates and offers available only to registered visitors.

Don't ask visitors for unnecessary information. It may be in their interest to give some details - to make sure they get the right offers, for example - but keep more detailed questions for later.

THE FIVE BUSINESS BENEFITS OF E-COMMERCE

4. PERSONALISATION

Personalisation: automated by site software.

Online channels are good at managing information in order to automate tasks. First, though, they need information to manage.

Many websites work by placing short text messages (cookies*) on the visitor's computer. Usually cookies exist only to track the site visit and to help the website recognise a visitor's computer (they won't know who is sitting at the keyboard unless the user chooses to reveal this information). Many cookies self-delete at the end of a browsing session.

Without cookies we would all find the internet much slower. However, some people are rightly concerned about their browsing information being captured and available for later use. It's important, therefore, to have a link to your privacy policy visible on every page.

When you return to this book's online site (see author's note at front) you'll see a *Welcome you@your email address* message. A cookie has recognised your computer and displays your group information.

 Cookies are short notes that websites make about their visitors, on the visitor's computer. On a PC look in c:Windows/cookies to see your cookies.

THE FIVE BUSINESS BENEFITS OF E-COMMERCE

4. PERSONALISATION

Customisation: by visitors to their preferences.

Visitors may wish to customise the pages that they see, to make them as useful as possible. However simple your company's product range, most of your customers will buy only some of your items. By personalising your page contents to their own preferences, visitors see only those products that are most relevant. Imagine, for example, a recipe book containing only your favourite foods plus some suggestions from the chef of similar dishes that you might like.

By searching for a cookie on the visitor's computer, the website can identify who is in touch and can then load the page that is in keeping with the visitor's requested information.

THE FIVE BUSINESS BENEFITS OF E-COMMERCE

4. PERSONALISATION

Personalisation is a win-win for customer and company.

If customers are able to put together their own orders, then personalisation will:

➤ Make it quicker and easier for the customer to buy in the future by showing only relevant products and by not asking for delivery and payment instructions to be re-entered.

➤ Make it less likely that customers will try out your competitors who offer less personalisation - or, even, the same personalisation opportunities - because they will have to enter their details again.

➤ Reduce the cost of managing your customer accounts, by giving them access to their account information and allowing them to carry out much of their own account management.

THE FIVE BUSINESS BENEFITS OF E-COMMERCE

5. GLOBAL REACH

If your company's products can be distributed globally, then e-commerce channels are an excellent and efficient way to exploit them:

➚ New customers and markets @ £0 incremental set-up costs

➚ 24 hour sales presence

➚ Distance is potentially irrelevant

➚ Smaller product niches become profitable when the niche expands globally

➚ Highly dispersed communities of customers can become closer to each other and to your organisation

Global reach
➎

THE FIVE BUSINESS BENEFITS OF E-COMMERCE

ACTION PLAN – QUESTIONS TO ADDRESS

Prioritise the 5 business benefits by answering these key questions:

- ↗ Where am I now regarding each benefit?
- ↗ What are my customers doing online now, at my website and at my competitors' sites?
- ↗ What impact will e-commerce have on my business in respect of:
  - reducing costs?
  - the flow of information to customers?
  - the flow of information from customers?
- ↗ What needs urgent attention and are these complementary activities?
- ↗ How far, and how fast, should developments be made?

NOTES

NEW THINKING FOR ONLINE BUSINESS

NEW THINKING FOR ONLINE BUSINESS

A SUMMARY OF THIS CHAPTER

- ↗ The customer now has more control
- ↗ The network economy's logic is different from that of the high street (but don't, of course, ignore business basics such as cashflow)
- ↗ Human attention is the rarest commodity
- ↗ Exploit online networks

NEW THINKING FOR ONLINE BUSINESS

THE CUSTOMER NOW HAS MORE CONTROL

In the *good old days*, your customers were at the end of a chain that began in a factory and ended when they collected goods from shops.

Now, the online customer sits at the centre of a circle and is able to reach any part of the old distribution chain in one step.

Being online gives customers much more choice over what they buy and much more control over who they buy from.

NEW THINKING FOR ONLINE BUSINESS

ON THE HIGH STREET MONEY DRIVES GROWTH

On the high street money is the currency that drives growth. To secure more customers, businesses spend money to invest in stock or production capacity in readiness for more new customers. And more money is spent on advertising, to attract more customers, and on providing more customer service to a larger number of customers.

Don't forget too that on the high street prime locations cost more.

NEW THINKING FOR ONLINE BUSINESS

ONLINE, VISITOR ATTENTION DRIVES GROWTH

Online, visitor attention drives the growth of your business, not money. There are three reasons for this:

1. Offline it costs money every time you communicate with your customers, whereas online this cost all but disappears. It is, therefore, less expensive to build customer loyalty online. And, as we all know, keeping an existing customer is more profitable than replacing a lost one.

2. Happy customers are likely to tell others of their buying experiences. Virtuous circles develop faster online because it's quick, inexpensive and easy to contact friends and colleagues. Web people call this *viral marketing*.

3. Once the first online shop is built for the first online customer, the running cost of providing the shop to customers number two through infinity is incrementally small and is proportional to each sale. Online businesses handle more orders for less processing cost and more profit.

NEW THINKING FOR ONLINE BUSINESS

HOW DOES A VIRAL CAMPAIGN START?

We spend our lives avoiding viruses, both those that affect us physically and those that affect our computers. But there is nothing wrong when your website has a healthy viral campaign running.

First, customers need to have a product or service that they want to recommend.

New levels of interaction, service and delivery are being achieved all the time. So set a new standard for customers that makes it easier to use your online channel rather than those of your competitors. Try one of these:

↗ The easiest - personalised - catalogue to browse

↗ Online ordering and account management facilities that customers can run themselves

↗ Put product manuals online where they can always be up-to-date

Now customers will tell friends about this service and they'll tell their friends, and it'll spread like a virus.

NEW THINKING FOR ONLINE BUSINESS

CREATING A VIRAL NETWORKING CAMPAIGN

OK, so you've created a new service. What now?
Expensive old economy thinking would be to invest money and promote it.

Instead of giving customers advertising to look at, give them something that costs the business virtually nothing and that customers will find useful.

Give away your new service.

In the old economy, companies charge more for products and services that are new and better. They charge a premium for the best.

When customers use the new service, they will bring in new customers. The more customers that use the service, the more new customers they will bring in. And sales will grow faster.

So *give it away*.

NEW THINKING FOR ONLINE BUSINESS

DID I SAY *GIVE IT AWAY?*

As in give it away for **free?** Not quite. But almost free.

Whatever service - or information - you're giving away, charge a small, token, price: one e-mail address.

Once that information is exchanged, the online customer network will start growing.

It works for newspapers, which give free access to their online editions, with a free archive search service. Customers may pay to retrieve the article they've found.

It works for retailers, who give customers a free store catalogue, online, and link it to free independent product reviews.

It works for courier services, which give customers the tools to track parcels and manage their own accounts.

And, of course, **it works for software companies**, which give away simple versions of their products and charge for fully-featured versions, or give away the full product and charge for support services.

NEW THINKING FOR ONLINE BUSINESS

DRIVING YOUR NETWORK TO GROW YOUR BUSINESS

Every person on one network is also part of other networks. At work there are colleagues, suppliers and customers, and away from the workplace we all have networks.

Once you've given away your new standard in order to build your network, how does the network grow?

Give away some more.

If the things that are given away are valuable to the network, then these people are likely to pay for the complementary services that a company charges for. Which means that the more you give away, the larger your network and the more you'll sell.

Remember to give away things that cost nothing to give away, cost next to nothing if one more customer uses them, and that build the network of paying customers.

NEW THINKING FOR ONLINE BUSINESS

BE FIRST IN A MARKETPLACE

Be first with an idea and it will spread more rapidly. Set a new standard in your marketplace and gain a reputation as an online leader. The formula is simple:

- ↗ Start small, try out ideas and move on quickly.
- ↗ Find out what customers like and use.
- ↗ Improve things regularly, a little at a time.
- ↗ Being first is important (but not essential). The fastest, smallest and smartest products have a short shelf life. Next week, somebody else will be faster, smaller or smarter.
- ↗ But first is always first. First mover advantage (webspeak again) gives your competitors another hurdle to overcome just to keep up.

NEW THINKING FOR ONLINE BUSINESS

THE NETWORK'S THE BEST JUDGE OF A GOOD IDEA

If you were allowed more than one smart idea, how many would you try?

As many as possible!

It is tough to know what customers will want, online or offline. And not every great idea is going to succeed. Give customers as many good ideas as possible - even not-quite-finished ideas. The web has created the Beta version - a nearly-finished idea that companies try out on customers. You can try it out too. Customers feel recognised and rewarded when asked to be involved in product development. You get free market testing.

Some ideas will turn out to be less-smart or too complex to finish, so drop them.

Note: If you're a car maker, please don't try Beta testing cars when the braking system isn't finished! The same health warning goes for all other products.

NEW THINKING FOR ONLINE BUSINESS

HOW TO STAY AHEAD OF ONLINE COMPETITION

The internet is a great way of developing a business. Sadly, the competition can benefit from it too. Like you, competitors just need a great idea and a network to sell into.

To stay in front of them become your own best competitor. Don't only look to improve your products, try to make them obsolete with even better new offerings.

Be prepared to let go of a product when it is at its most successful - and transfer its network to your new product.

NEW THINKING FOR ONLINE BUSINESS

HOW TO EXPLOIT ONLINE NETWORKS

Companies structure themselves around products:

- ↗ Management structure
- ↗ Production and sales teams
- ↗ Distribution channels

Customers don't think this way. Never have done, never will do.

Customers think about the end product. The meal, not the raw ingredients. Each individual product ingredient is a small part of the whole. Online, it is really easy to gather the whole buying experience onto one screen.

It's smarter, therefore, to organise online business around the way that customers think.

NEW THINKING FOR ONLINE BUSINESS

ORGANISING AROUND THE CUSTOMER: ONLINE MARKET SPACES

Usually we organise our businesses to reflect the physical world, and describe our companies as *business to business* or *business to consumer*. Online businesses don't have to follow this pattern.

Disintermediation* allows companies to change their place in the supply chain, so they're set up to service different types of customer.

The web lowers the cost to find, service, fulfil and retain customers. This makes less valuable customers profitable. Being online allows businesses to handle customers of almost any size or value. *All* to *All* trading becomes a practical reality.

 Disintermediation - literally *removing the intermediaries* - means that customers, retailers, distributors and manufacturers can all sell directly to each other. Traditionally, they were harnessed in a *supply chain*. Now customers can buy from anybody and everybody. Books, for example, can now be bought from the publisher, wholesalers, high street and online shops, and direct from the author. Through e-tailer's affiliate programmes it is even possible to buy a book from a reader.

NEW THINKING FOR ONLINE BUSINESS

THREE TYPES OF ALL TO ALL MARKETS

Businesses don't have to create their own market spaces online. Many already exist, tailored for different groups of customers. Remember, we're all customers now:

↗ Auction sites allow individuals to sell, bid and buy goods

↗ Collective trading permits individuals to combine to buy goods at volume prices

↗ *Pitch tents* enable businesses to invite tenders from suppliers:
- usually by invitation only
- and they may involve competitors joining together to invite tenders from suppliers; this grows the volumes and lowers the price for every participant

NEW THINKING FOR ONLINE BUSINESS

ACTION PLANNING 1

HOW CAN INFORMATION TRANSFER BETWEEN COMPANY & CUSTOMER BE IMPROVED?

- ↗ What information do customers need to provide?
- ↗ Could this information be more accurately and conveniently given online by customers?
- ↗ What information could the company give to its customers?
- ↗ What new information could be exchanged online?
- ↗ For each, is it a better service for customers?
- ↗ Is the new online service idea really compelling?
- ↗ Is it enough in itself to bring customers online, and to get them to start exchanging information?
- ↗ Will they tell friends and colleagues?

NEW THINKING FOR ONLINE BUSINESS

 ACTION PLANNING 2

WHERE IS THE BEST ONLINE BUSINESS OPPORTUNITY?

Can the company's online service be built around the customer?

- ↗ Their view of the company's products?
- ↗ Their view of complementary products?

When customers purchase the company's product, what else are they buying at the same time, from your company and from its competitors? What complementary goods are they buying to use with your products?

Is there an online marketplace where these goods are traded? Or can you share customers with those providing complementary services? Make it easier for customers to buy all the products they need to use with yours, by working with these other suppliers. For example, a customer buying pasta should be able to find all the ingredients for a complete meal: fresh vegetables for sauce or ready-made sauce, wine, dessert, coffee, candles, etc.

What does the company need to change to compete effectively in open market spaces?

NOTES

HOW TO PROMOTE A COMPANY ONLINE

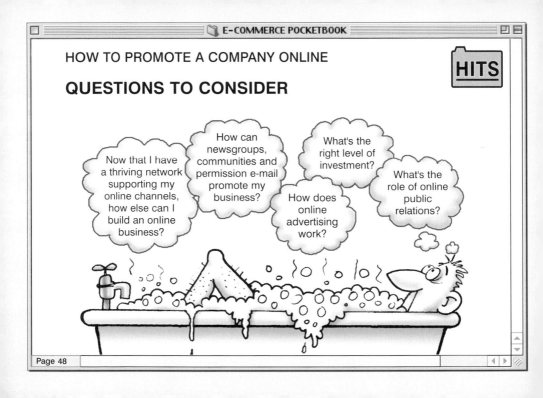

HOW TO PROMOTE A COMPANY ONLINE

HOW SHOULD YOUR COMPANY INVEST IN ONLINE COMMERCE?

There are 4 levels of company commitment to being online.

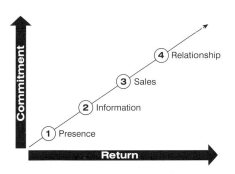

Customers don't yet know how they are going to use the online services that you offer them.

But online it's easier to see what works and what doesn't.

Expect to develop your services through rapid prototyping, development and obsolescence at each stage.

HOW TO PROMOTE A COMPANY ONLINE

LEVEL ONE: PRESENCE

HITS

Provide an online brochure. But don't simply transpose literature artwork to web pages. Online readers may be different from the people who read your printed literature. We all read differently online. Bear in mind:

- ↗ Fewer words will be required on each page, visible in a screen without the need to scroll
- ↗ Pictures take a long time to download, so smaller images may change page layouts
- ↗ We read books from cover to cover whereas online we follow the most interesting link in a non-linear structure

And don't forget to:

- ↗ Register the site with online directories and search engines
- ↗ Monitor traffic levels
- ↗ Put the web address on all printed stationery

HOW TO PROMOTE A COMPANY ONLINE

LEVEL TWO: INFORMATION

As a news and information service for all interested parties, your online channel should be responsive to customer questions and should permit registration for online communications.

When customers seek information from the website, there are different levels of technical sophistication to consider:

- Is the website linked to company databases? And are the links direct or indirect?

- Is there a one-way or two-way exchange of information? Can customers update their information?

- Is all of the information internal or can third parties supply useful information? Direct feeds from online news and weather services can add value for visitors who appreciate finding all the information they need in a single web page.

Above all, keep information pages up to date.

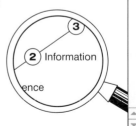

HOW TO PROMOTE A COMPANY ONLINE

LEVEL THREE: SALES

LESS FRICTION & MORE PROFIT ON EVERY SALE

Removing the cost of processing a sale online adds value to each sale.

Think of the *friction* caused whenever a human is involved in selling. What's *friction*? It is the cost of the time taken and resources used every time a piece of information has to be handled by a human being. There's no friction in a sale that is handled completely online.

It does cost a business to remove friction:

↗ There's the actual cost of installing and integrating computer programs

↗ The cost of managing the new roles that staff now play

↗ The cost of working with customers to get the new system right

Weigh up how much friction it's worth removing.

HOW TO PROMOTE A COMPANY ONLINE

LEVEL THREE: SALES

FRICTIONLESS SALES DEVELOPMENT IN THREE STEPS

A business does not have to become a complete dot.com overnight. Choose how much friction it is appropriate to remove:

1. e-service: friction-free self-service information

Customers can search in their own time for product and pricing information, press coverage and reviews. Online user manuals are always up-to-date.

2. e-commerce: friction-free transaction processing

An online front end to the existing business. Allow customers to assemble and pay for their orders online but use existing order handling systems for delivery.

3. e-business: friction-free order fulfilment and follow-up

Integrate all the processes into a single system in which all users of the system share the same information at the same time.

These tasks can be carried out in any order. Every step has back office and front office components. Back office systems can be integrated quietly in private, without changing the front office. Front office changes are more noticeable and may have PR advantages.

HOW TO PROMOTE A COMPANY ONLINE

LEVEL THREE: SALES

LOWER COSTS, NEW OPPORTUNITIES

Online channels can also reduce business overheads by:

 Reducing the print, storage and wastage costs of product literature and manuals

 Delivering information to customers, suppliers and distributors more quickly, at lower cost

 Allowing sales and distribution to develop with much lower capital (cash) investments

 Improving management reporting, at higher speed and accuracy

HOW TO PROMOTE A COMPANY ONLINE

LEVEL THREE: SALES

CATER FOR EVERYBODY, NOT JUST ONLINE CUSTOMERS

Since not all customers will wish to complete an order online, provide them with details of offline order systems.

Give these customers order forms that they can complete onscreen, print off and fax or post.

Make it easy for them to find your sales team's phone or fax number. Customers who don't wish to order online may still be happy to browse a catalogue and then call to place their orders.

HOW TO PROMOTE A COMPANY ONLINE

LEVEL FOUR: RELATIONSHIPS

With the three preceding levels of commitment taken on board, building relationships is the natural next level of commitment. Throughout online channels, buyers, sellers, suppliers and distributors share information with each other to create smarter businesses.

If this is a sensible thing to do, for everybody, then it's natural to wish to repeat it. And thus relationships are born.

So far, though, not many groups have hit this level. Moreover, technology is developing very quickly and with every development the idea of an online relationship changes. Today's relationship is next year's one night stand.

Your company and its online network will have to work out a definition of a relationship. **Together.**

HOW TO PROMOTE A COMPANY ONLINE

PERMISSION E-MAIL

HITS

There are *rules* to follow about how to e-mail your customers. A visitor (who, remember, is probably not yet a customer) gives his or her permission to receive e-mail when you have harvested their e-mail address (*harvesting* is described in 'The five business benefits of e-commerce'). But do not abuse that permission. Make it very clear that:

- Recipients control the relationship - why the e-mail has been sent
- It is easy to stop future communications - there will be no further follow-up
- E-mails are sent only once - make a strong statement that visitor information will remain private
- Recipients have the chance to update their information, and keep future e-mails relevant

When you follow all of these guidelines correctly, recipients will be happy to receive e-mail and will be more responsive.

HOW TO PROMOTE A COMPANY ONLINE

PERMISSION E-MAIL

The opposite of permission is *spam*.

Spam is the online term for unsolicited commercial e-mail (the legal definition) or 'e-mails that I didn't ask for, from people I don't know, selling products I don't want' (most people's definition of *spam*).

Guard against e-mail being treated as *spam* in three ways:

1. Legally   Does the use of customer information comply with relevant privacy legislation?

2. Rationally   Is customer information being used in the way the company intended and disclosed when it was first captured?

3. Emotionally   Will the recipients feel that they've been spammed?

HOW TO PROMOTE A COMPANY ONLINE

PERMISSION E-MAIL

There is no absolute definition of *spam*. Remember that the customer controls the relationship. If the customer says it's *spam*, then it is *spam*. Respect customer views.

It is *spam* when:

↗ The recipient's permission has 'decayed'. If it's been a while since permission was given, or since the last e-mail, the recipients may either have forgotten that they gave their permission or have withdrawn it.

↗ Permission is abused by writing too often.

The only defence against unintentionally *spamming* a customer is to have a clear and easy 'unsubscribe' link in every e-mail, and to make sure that customers who don't wish to receive e-mails never do.

HOW TO PROMOTE A COMPANY ONLINE

PERMISSION E-MAIL

KEEP E-MAILS ON MESSAGE

HITS

Once visitors understand who is writing to them, and are reminded that they gave their permission, your e-mail will be greeted more warmly. And warm e-mail is consistently better received than cold e-mail.

Building and maintaining the trust that you have built is vital. Keep your e-mails *on message*: if you received permission to write with service information for product owners, don't allow your e-mails to become a list of 'special' third-party offers.

HOW TO PROMOTE A COMPANY ONLINE

E-MAIL BASED ACTIVITY IS NOT ALL WORDS

HITS

Most of us use e-mail every day. We send simple text messages with documents attached. We might refer to a web page that the recipient should look at. Marketing e-mail should be as carefully prepared as any other communication.

Firstly, consider how the mail will be targeted. Domestic recipients, for instance, may not have high bandwidth connections and will not wish to receive large media-rich e-mails. Send them a simpler e-mail with a link to download the rich media content. Business to business recipients may be less restricted and can be sent larger messages.

Remember that while some televisions can receive e-mail, they may not be able to open attached documents and are rarely connected to a printer.

As with all measurable marketing activity, test different approaches and measure results to determine which is the most successful.

HOW TO PROMOTE A COMPANY ONLINE

THREE DIFFERENT TYPES OF E-MAIL

Text e-mail
- ↗ Stand-alone advertisements
- ↗ Sent to a list of people who have agreed to receive them
- ↗ Probably containing clickable links to *find out more* or to register for an offer

Visual e-mail
- ↗ Laid out in the form of a web page
- ↗ An effective way for a company to bring a website to its customers
- ↗ Can include graphics and banner advertising, so may generate advertising sales revenue while providing a service to customers

Rich Media by e-mail
- ↗ E-mail messages, sent through ordinary e-mail channels, that include graphics, sound, animation and video
- ↗ Can be personalised and can include HTML and rich media sounds or moving images

HOW TO PROMOTE A COMPANY ONLINE

HITS

SO YOU SEE WHAT I'M SAYING? – E-MAIL DESIGN

Recipients will have very slightly different display settings for their e-mail. Prepare e-mails so that they have the best chance of being displayed as the designer intended:

↗ Width of no more than 65 text characters
↗ Use white space and simple formatting to give fast download speeds
↗ Put unsubscribe information early in the message
↗ Build rapport and personalise by *speaking* one to one
↗ Demonstrate you know the customer's perspective

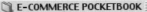
HOW TO PROMOTE A COMPANY ONLINE

COMPELLING E-MAIL COPY

HITS

Before the reader opens the message, the subject line, sender and, perhaps, the first lines of the message will be visible. Make these details enticing so that the message is opened:

- ↗ Place important information early in the message, before the reader has to scroll down

- ↗ Avoid *free* or hype language as some e-mail filter programs may block them

HOW TO PROMOTE A COMPANY ONLINE

USING E-MAIL SIGNATURES EFFECTIVELY

An e-mail signature at the end of a message is a powerful invitation for the reader to find out more.

- ↗ Create a suite of signatures for different purposes
- ↗ Be brief and to the point: 4-6 lines maximum, 60 characters in width
- ↗ Include contact information online and offline (an e-mail address and a relevant, clickable, URL) together with a brief benefit for the reader

For powerful business strategy e-mails
ReadyNow@SpotOnThinking.com
www.SpotOnThinking.com

HOW TO PROMOTE A COMPANY ONLINE

BUSINESS TO BUSINESS E-MAIL GUIDELINES

- ✗ Stick to brief text messages
- ✗ Avoid HTML for quicker downloads
- ✗ Research your lists; use test groups
- ✗ Offer something free if you can to generate leads
- ✗ Keep copy tight and to the point
- ✗ Put at least three response links in the copy - start, body copy and end
- ✗ Personalise as much as possible
- ✗ Give opportunities to ask questions, make comments, direct to a questionnaire, for example
- ✗ Speak to audience in their language, using their buzzwords
- ✗ Send out midweek and avoid busy periods
- ✗ Make sure you can respond to the response
- ✗ Then do it all again - follow-up mails can be as effective as the first communication

HOW TO PROMOTE A COMPANY ONLINE

HITS

ONLINE PUBLIC RELATIONS

A RESOURCE CENTRE FOR JOURNALISTS

Online, your public relations is a different job from traditional PR.

Activity can become highly interactive since the company is much closer to its customers and opinion formers.

Journalists work to tight deadlines. Press releases can get greater coverage by being available online, from where journalists can download extra, last-minute copy.

Provide editors and journalists with discrete areas of a company website. Give them the facility to download ASCII text versions of your press releases and to download low-, medium- and high- resolution photos to accompany stories.

HOW TO PROMOTE A COMPANY ONLINE

ONLINE PUBLIC RELATIONS

NEWSGROUPS & MESSAGE BOARDS

Joining and actively participating in a customer discussion list is a good way to meet key opinion-formers. Frank and open opinions are the engine of these online spaces, consequently they are very good for getting feedback on what customers think about your products. Journalists often use discussion lists for article research.

To get the best from discussion groups:

➤ Be clear about your objectives. Are you researching, publicising or informing and educating?

➤ Introduce yourself carefully: lurk and get a feel before being open about your interest in the group. Use an e-mail signature. Then subscribe and actively participate. **Share** expertise and knowledge with the group.

➤ Respect the culture and personalities within the group. Be prepared to apologise if you cause offence.

HOW TO PROMOTE A COMPANY ONLINE

FOUR FORMS OF ONLINE ADVERTISING

Advertising space can be bought from advertising sales houses, auction sites or bartered. There are four principal types of advert:

1. Text advertising - in text newsletters. Is there an e-mail newsletter for your industry? It may well carry text advertisement space which can be bought. Contact the list owner for details.

2. Banner ads - served in real time to the designated web page. Delivery is determined either by the advertisement's relevance to the viewer's interests or in rotation with other ads until a pre-arranged number of exposures is reached.

If your site has banner advertising space available it can be used as a very inexpensive way of sharing traffic. Exchange web space for visitors from other members of the banner exchange network or earn income by selling space to advertisers.

HOW TO PROMOTE A COMPANY ONLINE

FOUR FORMS OF ONLINE ADVERTISING

3. Pop-up windows - Interstitials in webspeak. Powerful communication if only because visitors have to click on the window to close it, so they may as well click the link in the ad and see what's there.

4. Superstitials - the pop-up window's grown-up sister. These windows have more media content. They may be interactive or they may play a video clip. As download speeds rise, these will become more common.

Don't forget to use your website address on every piece of print, from letterheads and business cards to advertising and product literature. It provides the most frequent opportunity to promote the site.

If the site has new services then say so alongside the web address.

HOW TO PROMOTE A COMPANY ONLINE

ACTION PLANNING

Make the company website visible offline:

➚ Put the address on every communication, from letterheads to advertising

➚ Find out how the company site could help journalists and public relations agents

Promote the company online. Identify no cost, low cost and paid promotion opportunities:

➚ Write and design for online communications

➚ Write interesting e-mails to customers but first ensure that they wish to receive them

➚ Make online graphics and copy messages consistent with all other media

➚ Measure the effectiveness of each initiative at bringing in valuable customers

NOTES

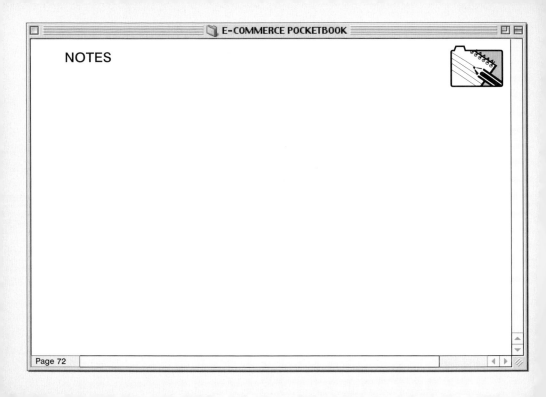

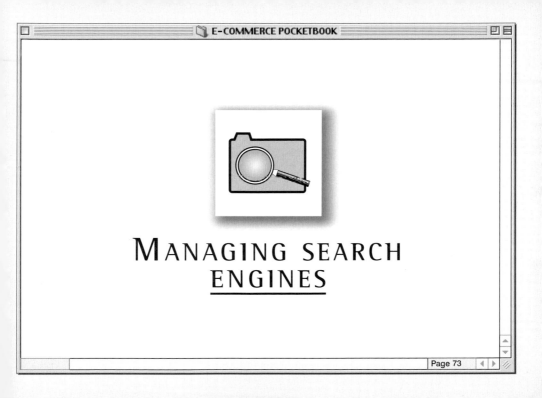

MANAGING SEARCH ENGINES

MANAGING SEARCH ENGINES

A FORMULA FOR SUCCESSFUL WEB SEARCHING

$$\left(\frac{\text{URL} + \text{Meta Tags (Page Title} + \text{Content} + \text{Description)}}{\text{Page Text} + \text{Image Alt Tags}}\right)^{\text{Recency}} = \boxed{\text{Your pages found!}}$$

MANAGING SEARCH ENGINES

GETTING THE BEST FROM SEARCH ENGINES

Search engines drive traffic to your web pages. They are the Yellow Pages of the internet. Estimates vary, and your site will have its own figures, but between 50% to 80% of traffic could come from the top ten major search engines.

Your site will need to be registered. There are three ways to do this:

↗ Wait for the search engine to find the company website by following a link from another site. This may take a very long time and is not recommended.

↗ Go to each search engine and select their *Submit URL* option, entering the required details.

↗ Use a human or software page submission service.

Whichever route is chosen, remember that while some search engines will index pages within days, others can take months or even a year to record a site. Normally indexing is free but several engines now offer a paid-for express service.

MANAGING SEARCH ENGINES

USING A URL TO PROMOTE YOUR COMPANY ONLINE

The UniqueResourceLocator is the address typed into a web browser's toolbar. Search engines will use it to answer their users' searches.

Your company name may be the first thing that visitors look for, therefore it makes sense to own 'yourcompanyname.yle*

Alternatively, visitors may type in what they are looking for and add yle to it. It is relatively quick and easy to register related URLs. A floor mop company might register, for example, FloorMop.yle, CleanFloors.yle and MrsMop.yle.

As soon as these are registered they can be directed at an existing company web page.

 .yle = your local extension

MANAGING SEARCH ENGINES

META TAGS HELP FIND TRAFFIC FOR YOUR SITE

What are they?

↗ HTML coded descriptions of site title, content and keywords

Why are they so important?

↗ Search engine spiders* use meta tags to identify relevance of your site to a search

↗ Search engines then compare the words in a search with the coded descriptions and with the page's content that details company products and services

View your page tags with *view source*: in Navigator and Explorer right click while viewing the web page for the correct menu or, in page editing software, view *page properties*.

 Spiders = software programs that run over web pages and index their contents

MANAGING SEARCH ENGINES

SEVEN IMPORTANT KEYWORD CONCEPTS

When writing keywords use terms that visitors searching for products will use, regardless of whether or not they know your company. Examples are from a floor mop company.

- ↗ Concepts   clean carpets, sparkling floor, hygienically clean floors
- ↗ Brands   product brand names (yours, not competitors)
- ↗ Company names   company name (current and previous names)
- ↗ Your name   well-known personnel - the chairman through to local sales representatives
- ↗ Common words   wax, polish, cloth, mop, cleaning fluid, etc
- ↗ Industry keywords   ISO standards, regulations, legislation, trade bodies
- ↗ Phrases   from advertising strap lines to the language used in company literature

Generic phrases are fine - hoover for example, even if it's not your trade name. But only use *970 Txi TurboSpeed* if it's one of your products.

MANAGING SEARCH ENGINES

FOUR WAYS TO MAKE KEYWORDS WORK FOR YOU

1. **Title:** include and repeat in the title of each page the keywords that people might search for to find the topic on that page.

2. **Prominence:** keywords that are more prominent will be weighted much higher by search engines. Most engines give higher rankings to keywords near the beginning of the title and to those that are close to the beginning of the page.

3. **Length of page:** keep your pages short. Repeat keywords frequently, particularly in the first 3-5 lines of the pages. Some engines ignore or largely ignore wording beyond the first paragraph or two.

4. **Observe and experiment:** use activity log files to understand which keywords work best with each search engine.

MANAGING SEARCH ENGINES

FOUR TIPS TO AVOID MISTAKES IN PAGE DESIGN

1. **Repetition:** never repeat a keyword more than 6-7 times on a page.

2. **Avoid frames:** not all spiders (eg: Altavista's) will follow links that are in frames.

3. **Provide a link back to the home page:** the first page your visitors find is unlikely to be your home page. Always place a link back to your home page.

4. **First impressions count:** most search engines will display the first few lines of text. Summarise contents in those first few lines.

MANAGING SEARCH ENGINES

USE PAGE TEXT TO SUPPORT META TAGS

Now that it has read your meta tags, the search engine will compare them with the words on the web page. Most engines read at least the first seven to ten lines of text.

Make the engine's life easy. Put as many of the meta tag words and phrases into your opening paragraphs as possible. A higher correlation between meta tags and copy will get a higher ranking.

The challenge, of course, is to include as many tags as possible without making the opening paragraphs read as if they were written by a five-year-old. There is a skill in this. But look at the web pages that top search results - chances are, they've made a success of it.

MANAGING SEARCH ENGINES

GATEWAY PAGES POINT THE WAY

The more information that is crammed into a single web page, the less importance a search engine will attach to each topic on the page.

Describe in equal lengths five products on the same page and each will receive one fifth of the engine's weighting. Put fifty products on the same page and each will receive just 2% weighting (not much!).

If your company has many products it will pay to create individual product pages and to register main product groups separately with search engines.

MANAGING SEARCH ENGINES

ALT TAGS TURN PICTURES INTO WORDS

Search engine spiders can't see pictures. They rely on alt tags - a few words that describe the image - to tell them what is in the picture. View them by placing the cursor over a picture: if a short line of text appears after a few seconds, that's the alt tag.

Tell the search engine what's in the picture. If it's a company logo, don't use *company logo* as the alt tag. This is meaningless.

Give the engine something to work with: *Brasso widgets, quality brass widgets to buy online* is good, especially if all these words are in your page meta tags.

MANAGING SEARCH ENGINES

LEARN FROM YOUR COMPETITORS

Try using search engines to find your own site. How easy is it? If competitors are placed higher in searches, take a look at their pages and meta tags. What have they done to merit a higher ranking? Don't forget to view the websites of your international competitors, too.

Check the server log files: what are the most popular search terms used to find your site? Try out those searches and check out any pages ranking above your own.

MANAGING SEARCH ENGINES

ONCE A PAGE IS WELL RANKED ...
KEEP IT THERE

Engines re-visit web pages to find out if they have changed.
The more often they change, the more often they are visited.
And engines' results lists usually
reflect how recently a
page was up-dated.

Up-date pages regularly.

MANAGING SEARCH ENGINES

AND FINALLY, MOMENTUM

Many search engines favour sites that rank highly in previous searches and that were clicked upon.

The better the rankings a site achieves, the more the engine will do to keep it at this level. This makes it tougher to break into the top results. But once a page makes it to the top, it will be more visible in search results, be visited more often and quickly becomes harder to dislodge.

Get a page up there. The effort repays itself.

MANAGING SEARCH ENGINES

 # ACTION PLANNING

- ↗ Is the site designed to be search-engine friendly?
- ↗ Are meta tags and alt tags in place?
  - Check that they are the right tags for your company.
  - Search for a meta tag generator if you're not sure.
- ↗ Is the site registered with major search engines?
  - Search for the site. If it's not top of the search, find out what your higher placed competitors did to earn their ranking.
  - Make some improvements. Try changing one thing on each page.
  - Measure what effect this has by reading the log files.

NOTES

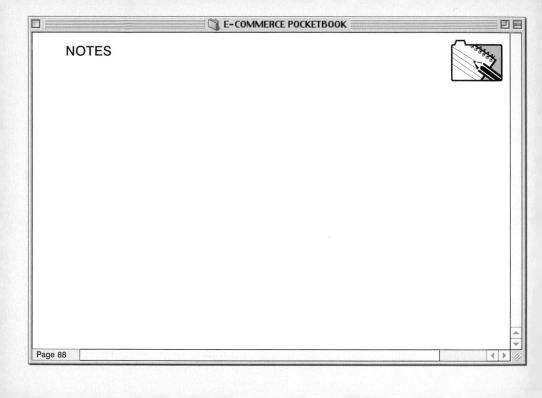

CREATING TRUST:
SECURITY & DATA PROTECTION

CREATING TRUST: SECURITY & DATA PROTECTION

MAKE YOUR SECURITY APPROPRIATE

Every website needs the right level of security for the information that is being protected. A dime widget store needs a lot less security than a bank.

Ensure that customers do not feel inhibited, delayed or inconvenienced by any security process. But do protect yourself from customers.

↗ What level of encryption do you need?

↗ How do your customers know that they are looking at your web pages? And how does your website know that customers are who they say they are?

↗ What information do you have if a customer says they did not make an order or the goods were not delivered?

CREATING TRUST: SECURITY & DATA PROTECTION

SECURE YOUR SITE INTERNALLY & EXTERNALLY

Worldwide most web users have access to 128 bit encryption versions of their web browsers. This was until recently banking-level security. It is, therefore, likely to be good enough for any transactions a company will ask its customers to make.

Most payments take place behind a Secure Socket Layer - the locked padlock browser area. This is usually a more heavily firewalled area of your web server.

A website's biggest security threat may not come from outside your organisation. Research shows that most security breaches are internal. Consequently, you should ensure that internal controls are installed alongside an external firewall.

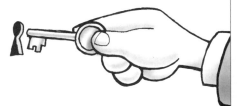

CREATING TRUST: SECURITY & DATA PROTECTION

WEBSITE & VISITOR VERIFICATION

Do you know who you're talking to? It is relatively easy to become anonymous online or to assume a different persona. Malicious people may even temporarily steal a site's identity.

It is important to be able to authenticate that a website is what it claims to be and visitors are genuinely who they say they are. Site verification can be carried out by Verisign or other similar organisations. By a process of cross-verification, visitors can check that a site is *what it claims to be*.

The simplest way for a website to confirm that customers are genuine is to have a system of user identification - usually passwords and personal data that customers enter to identify themselves.

More and more personal digital certificates are being issued. These allow websites to verify that visitors are *who they say they are* before allowing purchases to be made.

CREATING TRUST: SECURITY & DATA PROTECTION

CUSTOMER TRANSACTION RECORDS

Since the dawn of time mail order companies have struggled with customers who claim that something was missing from their order. Online services have the extra headache of customers claiming that goods have been charged to their accounts in error.

The advantage of online sales records is that they are complete records of customers' transactions. They may even contain other information about a customer's activity in the lead up to the purchase process.

Records are also, of course, electronic. They can be traced and can confirm that purchases were made, on which dates and by whom.

Log files from the secure order areas of a site should be kept. These should contain more detail than other traffic reports and should be held for longer.

CREATING TRUST: SECURITY & DATA PROTECTION

TRUST

Trust is a dynamic process for most consumers. Trust deepens or retreats depending on our experiences of dealing with suppliers. It's the same online as in the high street, though online we only have the images on an electronic screen to judge a company by.

Before we trust an organisation, we look for rational and emotional indicators.

↗ Emotionally, we look for behaviours such as manners, professionalism and sensitivity.

↗ Rationally, formal claims to trustworthiness such as dependability, reliability and honesty reassure us.*

And we look for visible signs of security.

 Source: Cheskin Research

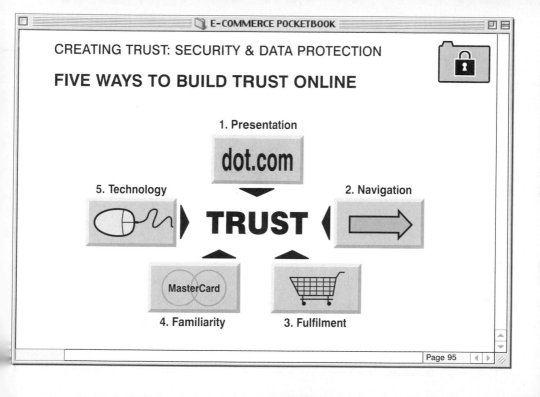

CREATING TRUST: SECURITY & DATA PROTECTION

FIVE WAYS TO BUILD TRUST ONLINE

1. PRESENTATION

The look of a site conveys a sense of personality and influences the degree to which visitors are prepared to trust the site owner.

If an organisation already has a corporate identity then the site should be consistent with this. On-screen design and copy styles should reflect existing printed literature. A company's colours may need re-working online, to a new palette that is fast to download to the computer screen.

Developing a brand to work online is a new task. The internet is tactile - web pages should look, sound and move in ways that reinforce the company's existing image.

CREATING TRUST: SECURITY & DATA PROTECTION

FIVE WAYS TO BUILD TRUST ONLINE

2. NAVIGATION

If customers walk into a new high street shop they can usually find their way around. There are conventions for laying out a shop and customers unconsciously understand and follow them.

Online conventions are still being developed. Therefore, some judgement will be needed to make first-time visits successful. The challenge is to create enticement - to explore the store - without customers getting lost.

On the home page a site's purpose must be clear to the first-time visitor. Use simple words to describe the site's content and make it easy for visitors to find what they are looking for by giving clear instructions. Follow the most common layout conventions:

- ↗ Navigation links at top and bottom of pages
- ↗ Images and buttons in the same place on each page
- ↗ Text hyperlinks underlined in blue

CREATING TRUST: SECURITY & DATA PROTECTION

FIVE WAYS TO BUILD TRUST ONLINE

3. FULFILMENT

Goods have now been selected and your customer has made it to the checkout. At this point most shopping carts are abandoned.

Websites can keep customers' trust by taking them through a transparent transaction process. At all times customers should know where they are in the checkout process and they should be able to find out what happens later. It must be easy to see:

↗ How orders are to be processed

↗ The company's returns policy

↗ Online and offline customer support services

↗ The company's security policy for personal information

If you have shops on the high street, give customers the option to return goods there. And remember to train your staff to handle returned online orders.

CREATING TRUST: SECURITY & DATA PROTECTION

FIVE WAYS TO BUILD TRUST ONLINE

4. FAMILIAR NAMES & LOGOS

Names that we know and trust are familiar and friendly. If we see them on a website we trust the website more.

Customers trust sites where they can see the familiar logos of credit card brands, major software companies and web security organisations. If your company is trusted by these organisations, don't hide it.

Should your company have a familiar name, use it to build customer expectation of the site's content, the quality of products and the level of service support. Web customers will have higher service expectations than offline customers. They may expect service delivered in real time, with transparency and, above all, with **consistency**.

CREATING TRUST: SECURITY & DATA PROTECTION

FIVE WAYS TO BUILD TRUST ONLINE

5. TECHNOLOGY

Too much technology can be daunting. Use technology as a transparent aid to navigation and activity. Aim for graphics and functions in proportion to your customer's needs. These needs will change with your customer's experience.

- ↗ Are you handling visitors *new to the web* trade or devotees?
    - Newcomers need signposts and easy navigation.
    - Old hands need quick routes to every part of the site.
- ↗ Younger visitors and technically aware customers may be more tolerant of higher technical demands.

Make sure that technology supports your sales process and does not obscure it:

- ↗ Automatically recognise returning customers
- ↗ Help to complete forms correctly
- ↗ Design forms to work with software programs that automatically add user details to the form

CREATING TRUST: SECURITY & DATA PROTECTION

SIX WAYS TO LOSE CUSTOMER TRUST

Make these mistakes and your customers will disappear fast:

1. Make public a customer's personal details.

2. Re mail your customer's personal files (usually to other customers).

3. Allow your site to be spoofed. A close copy of your site can undermine the genuine article.

4. Permit a determined hacker to change your web pages.

5. Transmit customer information over the internet without encryption, where it can be detected, collected and misused.

6. Allow transactions to be intercepted and altered en-route. Customer names, credit card numbers and payment values are vulnerable.

CREATING TRUST: SECURITY & DATA PROTECTION

CYBERSQUATTING & CLAIMING YOUR OWN NAME

Your domain name is a valuable property. Don't allow anybody to steal it from you. There is now legal precedent in many countries to protect *yourcompanyname.yle.* But, of course, there will be more than one legitimate claimant to many names.

Ask nicely for your chosen name if it is taken. The owner may quote a small price (or a large one!) to transfer the name.

If you have a strong claim to a name, and the owner will not release it, consider referring the matter to the World Intellectual Property Organisation (WIPO). For a fee of $1,000 to $3,500 (US) WIPO will judge who holds the right to a name.

CREATING TRUST: SECURITY & DATA PROTECTION

DATA PROTECTION

Terrestrial data protection legislation often now applies to personal data gathered from online sources.

Take the European Community as a model. Their view is that sites should comply with the *native* data protection legislation.

For example, in the case of a site owned by a German company, the courts would expect personal data to be handled in compliance with German laws. This would apply:

↗ Even if the site were hosted in another country

↗ Regardless of which country had the more strict data protection regulations

There are, of course, many local variations and frequent changes. Please check with a local lawyer.

CREATING TRUST: SECURITY & DATA PROTECTION

PERSONAL & IMPERSONAL DATA

Most data protection legislation is framed on the assumption that a name or address is an essential part of the collection process. Once one of these details is attached to a profile, in law it becomes *personal*.

Impersonal data about visitors can be collected when they visit websites, wap sites or interactive television channels. This form of data gathering is not yet covered by specific legislation. However, it soon will be because of the scale and scope of the information that can be gathered.

CREATING TRUST: SECURITY & DATA PROTECTION

COLLECTING & USING IMPERSONAL DATA AT A SINGLE SITE

Online, a name or even an e-mail address is not essential to build up a profile.

Tracking an individual visitor during a visit to a website can build an informative profile of their interests. This is unlikely to cause offence if the details are not attached to information from other sources.

It is relatively easy to:

- ↗ Inform your visitors of the tracking that is carried out on a company site
- ↗ Explain the advantages
- ↗ Seek permission to use tracking information to personalise users' visits

CREATING TRUST: SECURITY & DATA PROTECTION

COLLECTING & USING DATA OVER A NETWORK OF SITES

In the same way that a visitor can be tracked within a single site, advertising networks can follow browsers across a number of websites and build a profile of their interests. Over time, a highly detailed profile will be assembled. This is very powerful because it is based on what we *actually* do online.

Advertisers use this technology to deliver banner advertising that they think will be of most interest to the visitor. Advertisement targeting can be based on an individual's browsing habits and built anonymously over a period of time without the individual's permission.

Browsers benefit from being shown more relevant advertising in the sites that they visit. Whole web pages can be constructed for each individual visitor, based on their browsing habits. Clearly this has the potential to cause upset, as it may feel like an invasion of privacy. It is not yet covered in law.

CREATING TRUST: SECURITY & DATA PROTECTION

ACTIONS TO PROTECT DATA THAT IS GATHERED ONLINE

The Network Advertising Initiative is developing self-regulatory principles to protect consumer privacy and inspire trust. The initiative will provide sound guidelines for any company that has the opportunity to collect visitor data from online channels.

- Companies must not sell information collected from cookies to third parties.
- Nor must they track sensitive information such as medical information and financial information (creditworthiness).
- Companies should provide consumers with notice and choice about internet advertising.
- They must disclose their data collection and use practices on their websites in a clear, concise and conspicuous manner. They must disclose:
  - What visitor information was captured and subsequently retained or deleted
  - How data is used
  - What opt-in or opt-out procedures are available to the visitor

CREATING TRUST: SECURITY & DATA PROTECTION

WHEN IS A LEGAL CONTRACT MADE ONLINE?

When an order is placed online the customer will expect that order to hold the same legal status as an order that is placed via a sales representative or mailed/faxed direct to the supplier.

In fact, that's not necessarily so. There is a delay, however small, between clicking the *send* button at the electronic checkout and the order being received. And there is a delay, however small, in the order being confirmed by the seller. As these communications travel across the internet, there is a chance that they could be deflected or altered. Legally, there is some room for doubt that an order or acknowledgement was sent or received by the intended recipient.

Legal systems vary from country to country. None of them, though, is likely to incorporate contract law that was written to accommodate e-commerce. Check on the local rules and their interpretations if, indeed, there are *any* interpretations.

CREATING TRUST: SECURITY & DATA PROTECTION

 # ACTION PLANNING

LEGAL ISSUES

The law is coming to terms with e-commerce at a different rate in each country. Although the web is global, judgements vary from one jurisdiction to another. Ask your local legal advisers for their views.

- ↗ Who is responsible for what is said in a chat room? If it is the people chatting, who are they? Or does the company that provides the chat space publish its content and take responsibility?

- ↗ What rights and responsibilities do employers have for the contents of employees' computers?

- ↗ In a global communications medium, which advertising law applies? In Europe, the policy is that advertising and products from European companies must comply with domestic legislation.

- ↗ Is the company registered for the appropriate data protection legislation?

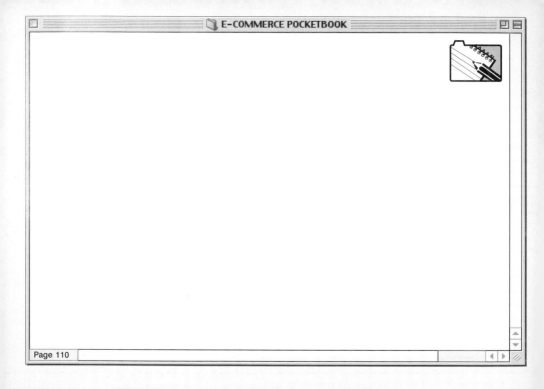

EIGHT STEPS TO PLAN SUCCESSFUL E-COMMERCE

EIGHT STEPS TO PLAN SUCCESSFUL E-COMMERCE

❶ LET THE CUSTOMER PLAN E-COMMERCE

Good plans are simple plans. They are also measurable, their implementation is accountable, the resources to deliver the plan are available and there is a time-frame for the plan to be delivered.

Done.

Not quite. Whatever planning process an organisation uses, expect that the company will not control the direction in which online services evolve. The customer will decide what works and what doesn't.

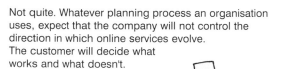

EIGHT STEPS TO PLAN SUCCESSFUL E-COMMERCE

❷ RESPOND FAST

If the plan is to respond to customer wishes, then the most successful plan will be the one that responds fastest.

This means that every component of the plan should be built with the intention of proving a principle.

Ask yourself if your customers want this?

If they do, then a more robust version can be built.

If they don't, then you can redirect your time and resources and use the knowledge gained to good effect elsewhere.

EIGHT STEPS TO PLAN SUCCESSFUL E-COMMERCE

❸ TEST OUT YOUR PLAN

In the online marketplace everything is a test until it's proven by the customer.

Successful testing follows a simple rule:

Test one thing at a time.

Only test changes that can be measured directly. If a test includes more than one change, it's almost always impossible to measure the effect of each one.

Test to learn from the customer and to improve one step at a time.

EIGHT STEPS TO PLAN SUCCESSFUL E-COMMERCE

❹ CHALLENGE INTERNAL ASSUMPTIONS

Remove internal processing costs to make dramatic improvements to profit margins.

Analyse each sales process to clarify what it is that staff spend time doing. In particular, look for processes in which information is transferred.

↗ How many steps can be eliminated by outsourcing tasks to your customers and suppliers?

↗ Who is best placed to make the original information entry?

↗ Can that information be shared to avoid re-entering the same information?

↗ What information could customers, suppliers and distributors find for themselves, computer to computer?

↗ With the time saved, what could your staff do to add more value for customers?

EIGHT STEPS TO PLAN SUCCESSFUL E-COMMERCE

❺ FOCUS ON CUSTOMER, SUPPLIER & DISTRIBUTOR BENEFITS

What's in it for customers, suppliers and distributors? Have you asked what they'd like? The web's very good at research. Are you offering them a new way to use an existing service or a completely new service? Is it faster, cheaper, more convenient or just new and online? What new information do they get?

Decide what you can reliably offer each group now and plan a phased introduction of more complex services. Complexity often arises from integrating tried and tested stand-alone services.

EIGHT STEPS TO PLAN SUCCESSFUL E-COMMERCE

❻ GIVE GOOD REASONS TO USE ONLINE SERVICES

Not all customers will automatically move to an online service simply because it's there. Equally, in a service's early stages it may not make good sense to risk overwhelming a new online channel by quickly moving large numbers of customers over to the new service.

If you prefer customers to use an online channel, find ways to:

↗ Inform them that it is there (they may not know this)

↗ Tell them how to change over

↗ Incentivise the swap to make it worthwhile

↗ Introduce the new service as a special privilege beta test programme

EIGHT STEPS TO PLAN SUCCESSFUL E-COMMERCE

❼ CALCULATE THE THREE SETS OF COSTS

Very few organisations have all the resources in-house to start offering online services.

There are three sets of costs that should be calculated:

1. Current company costs that will be altered by the online changes
   - both internal and external costs

2. Cost to implement the changes
   - interim support may be needed
   - training for staff whose tasks change

3. New cost assumptions, post change
   - long-term cost-savings
   - long-term outsourcing arrangements
   - ongoing online development plans

EIGHT STEPS TO PLAN SUCCESSFUL E-COMMERCE

❽ HELP STAFF ADAPT TO ONLINE WORKING

An online service will affect your staff and the work that they do.

If your organisation is typical, there will be a progressive transfer from processing tasks towards customer service. Some may find this work more fulfilling; others will not enjoy the increased interaction with customers.

Unless a company's online services are entirely online, staff who are to fulfil new service roles will require assistance to develop new skills. They will almost certainly require some training in how to make the most of the new technology for the benefit of their customers.

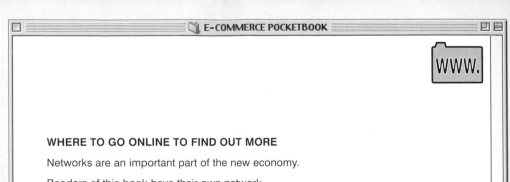

WHERE TO GO ONLINE TO FIND OUT MORE

Networks are an important part of the new economy.

Readers of this book have their own network.

Join us at *www.ecommercepocketbook.com*

It's a space in which you can share with other managers around the world your ideas, experiences and the challenges of managing e-commerce.

About the Author

Will Rowan

Will is an experienced e-commerce consultant and trainer, with roots in blue-chip direct marketing. Since 1998 his consultancy TheCustomer.co.uk has provided new marketing technologies training and consultancy to top five UK direct marketing agencies, leading travel and travel incentive companies, major banks, building societies, insurers, educational bodies and recruitment organisations.

Clients use TheCustomer.co.uk for practical advice in exploiting new network technologies to make businesses more profitable:

- Strategic advice to business on the consequences of new technologies for customer communications and company structure

- Restructuring companies, communications and customer service activities to profit from customer information

- Identifying opportunities to improve business processes by applying customer information in real time

Will lives on the edge of the New Forest where he cycles, walks and occasionally works from a highly portable office. Readers may reach Will at Ask@TheCustomer.co.uk

THE MANAGEMENT POCKETBOOK SERIES

Pocketbooks

Appraisals Pocketbook
Assertiveness Pocketbook
Balance Sheet Pocketbook
Business Planning Pocketbook
Business Presenter's Pocketbook
Business Writing Pocketbook
Challengers Pocketbook
Coaching Pocketbook
Communicator's Pocketbook
Controlling Absenteeism Pocketbook
Creative Manager's Pocketbook
Cross-cultural Business Pocketbook
Cultural Gaffes Pocketbook
Customer Service Pocketbook
Decision-making Pocketbook
Empowerment Pocketbook
Export Pocketbook
Facilitator's Pocketbook
Improving Efficiency Pocketbook
Improving Profitability Pocketbook
Induction Pocketbook
Influencing Pocketbook

Interviewer's Pocketbook
Key Account Manager's Pocketbook
Learner's Pocketbook
Managing Budgets Pocketbook
Managing Cashflow Pocketbook
Managing Change Pocketbook
Managing Your Appraisal Pocketbook
Manager's Pocketbook
Manager's Training Pocketbook
Marketing Pocketbook
Meetings Pocketbook
Mentoring Pocketbook
Motivation Pocketbook
Negotiator's Pocketbook
Networking Pocketbook
People Manager's Pocketbook
Performance Management Pocketbook
Personal Success Pocketbook
Project Management Pocketbook
Problem Behaviour Pocketbook
Quality Pocketbook
Sales Excellence Pocketbook
Salesperson's Pocketbook

Self-managed Development Pocketbook
Stress Pocketbook
Teamworking Pocketbook
Telephone Skills Pocketbook
Telesales Pocketbook
Thinker's Pocketbook
Time Management Pocketbook
Trainer Standards Pocketbook
Trainer's Pocketbook

Pocketfiles/Other

Leadership: Sharing The Passion
The Great Presentation Scandal
Hook Your Audience
Trainer's Blue Pocketfile of
Ready-to-use Exercises
Trainer's Green Pocketfile of
Ready-to-use Exercises
Trainer's Red Pocketfile of
Ready-to-use Exercises

Audio Cassettes

Tips for Presenters
Tips for Trainers

ORDER FORM

Your details

Name _____

Position _____

Company _____

Address _____

_____

Telephone _____

Facsimile _____

E-mail _____

VAT No. (EC companies) _____

Your Order Ref _____

Please send me:

			No. copies
The	E-commerce	Pocketbook	
The		Pocketbook	
The		Pocketbook	
The		Pocketbook	
The		Pocketbook	

Order by Post

MANAGEMENT POCKETBOOKS LTD
14 EAST STREET ALRESFORD HAMPSHIRE SO24 9EE UK

Order by Phone, Fax or Internet

Telephone: +44 (0)1962 735573
Facsimile: +44 (0)1962 733637
E-mail: pocketbks@aol.com
Web: www.pocketbook.co.uk

Customers in USA should contact:
Stylus Publishing, LLC, 22883 Quicksilver Drive,
Sterling, VA 20166-2012
Telephone: 703 661 1581 or 800 232 0223
Facsimile: 703 661 1501 E-mail: styluspub@aol.com